AN ILLUSTRATED BOOK OF

LOADED LANGUAGE

ALI ALMOSSAWI

ILLUSTRATIONS BY
Alejandro Giraldo

THE EXPERIMENT

NEW YORK

The Experiment, LLC | 220 East 23rd Street, Suite 600 | New York, NY 10010-4658
theexperimentpublishing.com

THE EXPERIMENT and its colophon are registered trademarks of The Experiment, LLC. Many of the designations used by manufacturers and sellers to distinguish their products are claimed as trademarks. Where those designations appear in this book and The Experiment was aware of a trademark claim, the designations have been capitalized.

The Experiment's books are available at special discounts when purchased in bulk for premiums and sales promotions as well as for fundraising or educational use. For details, contact us at info@theexperimentpublishing.com.

Library of Congress Cataloging-in-Publication Data available upon request

ISBN 978-1-61519-840-5
Ebook ISBN 978-1-61519-841-2

Cover design by Beth Bugler
Text design by Jack Dunnington
Illustrations by Alejandro Giraldo

Manufactured in the United States of America

First printing November 2021
10 9 8 7 6 5 4 3 2 1

To my father

CONTENTS

A QUICK INTRODUCTION: THE SUBTLE WAYS
LANGUAGE INFLUENCES THOUGHT   1

1. LANGUAGE THAT CONCEALS
    WITH VAGUENESS   6

2. LANGUAGE THAT CREATES
    SINISTER ASSOCIATIONS   19

3. LANGUAGE THAT CREATES
    FEEL—GOOD ASSOCIATIONS   29

4. LANGUAGE THAT PRESUPPOSES   42

5. LANGUAGE THAT FEIGNS OBJECTIVITY   50
    WITH APPARENT NEUTRALITY

6. LANGUAGE THAT STARTS THE CLOCK OF   61
    HISTORY WHEN IT'S MOST CONVENIENT

7. LANGUAGE THAT TELLS YOU HOW   72
    TO THINK ABOUT YOURSELF

FINAL REMARKS   82

SUGGESTED READING & SOURCES   85

ACKNOWLEDGMENTS   87

ABOUT THE AUTHOR AND ILLUSTRATOR   88

That the very concept of objective truth is
fading out of the world . . . frightens me
much more than bombs.

—*George Orwell*

A QUICK INTRODUCTION:
THE SUBTLE WAYS LANGUAGE INFLUENCES THOUGHT

Oh hello! Mr. Rabbit here. I'm pleased to meet you. You might be wondering how I've reached this, ahem, honorable old age. I'll tell you: Careful listening is essential for a rabbit—and today, sneaky language is more prevalent than ever. It's prevalent in everyday conversations, in newspapers and websites of record, in posts shared by influential people, and in speeches by eloquent intellectuals. It colors how we perceive our world. You're holding a compendium of this kind of rhetoric—not only what's said out loud, but also what's left unsaid.

One reason rhetorical sleight of hand gets past us is that, when listening to someone speak, we tend to focus on whether we *like* that person rather than whether they are making any sense. Another reason is that our brains, by nature, process information differently based on context. Consider two well-known effects:

Priming. In a video that made the rounds online, a fun-loving group is sitting in a living room. Without showing any visuals, one of them asks another—an English major, no less—to pronounce T-W-A, which she does phonetically. He asks her to pronounce T-W-I, which she does, the same way. Then onto T-W-O, at which point her increasingly peculiar attempts leave everyone in stitches. Other videos of that sort of gag are aplenty.

What's interesting here is that our English major is using instincts that normally serve her well to try to answer a seemingly simple question. But, the information she's given at the start proves debilitating as she attempts to reason through what follows, all to great comedic effect. People are sensitive to what came just before!

Framing. In the classic example of framing, two groups of participants were asked to choose between two treatments for an imaginary disease that is about to kill 600 people:

Group 1 chose between A) a treatment that saves 200 people, and B) a treatment with a one-third chance of saving all 600 and a two-thirds chance of saving no one.

Group 2 chose between A) a treatment that causes 400 people to die, and B) a treatment with a two-thirds chance of causing all 600 to die and a one-third chance of causing no one to die.

Both sets of choices are equivalent, but in Group 1, given the positive framing, more participants chose the treatment with the certain outcome, A. In Group 2, given the negative framing, more participants chose the treatment with the riskier outcome, B.

These examples and many others show that our judgment, our instincts, our reflexes—which we rely on for so much of our daily decision-making—aren't as reliable as we think. We're susceptible to how information is packaged and presented to us. Cognitive bias—and social bias—creeps in.

Our biases—optical illusions, in effect—number in the tens or hundreds depending on whom you ask, and many are subtle. For instance, grouping countries by location *feels* natural, as does sorting things alphabetically. Yet these instincts are far from natural—they are in fact man-made. It's this type of bias, in particular, that made me want to share this guide with you.

In the next seven sections, and accompanied by memorable illustrations (some of me!), I consider how the language we craft and consume shapes our beliefs. I'm primarily interested in language that *manipulates*, for example by creating sinister associations, concealing with vagueness, or feigning objectivity with apparent neutrality. My categories will overlap, and my chosen examples aren't meant to be exhaustive.

Not all "loaded language" is intentionally devious: While some writers aim to mislead us, others may use it unwittingly—especially when implicit bias comes into play. When a journalist refers to a politician's *fact-free rhetorical style* rather than his *lies*, she more likely seeks to entertain than to excuse. A good many of my examples are from sources generally considered to be neutral, unbiased, and nonpartisan. I try to lay any implicit bias bare.

Rhetoric—*how* someone says something—can offer useful insight into their underlying assumptions. But note that I won't focus on evolving constructs like political correctness, or lazily exploitable ones like identity politics. I don't discuss language that's obviously bigoted or insincere (which I trust my discerning readers will recognize on their own)! I also leave the important topic of how someone's culture informs their interpretation of language—since, after all, English speakers come from a wealth and breadth of cultures—to the relevant experts.

This guide is about the *words* used to talk about various issues, and not about the issues themselves. You humans have a divisive-enough political climate as it is; I don't intend to contribute to it! To that end, I have adapted certain examples taken from real-world media to feature rabbits and badgers. A select few have been slightly embellished for comedic effect.

Any connection between badgers and the wrongheaded side of things is purely coincidental.

IT'S BEAUTIFUL, ISN'T It?
HIS MAJESTY'S CLOTHES-FREE SARTORIAL STYLE.

1. LANGUAGE THAT CONCEALS WITH VAGUENESS

Vagueness is at the heart of insincere language; it clouds thinking and it muddies meaning. As Orwell writes about vague terms, "The person who uses them has his own private definition, but allows his hearer to think he means something quite different."

Vague language is often used to dissociate someone (perhaps we ourselves?) from a contemptible act or bad memory. In a classic moral thought experiment, a runaway trolley will strike and kill five people—unless you flip a switch to divert it, in which case it will kill one person. All things being equal, the math is simple, but it feels more comfortable to cause harm *indirectly* than to take action (by flipping the switch) and become complicit. We see that same instinct at work with vague language.

Let's look at some examples.

Misattributing actions. Objects can sometimes take on a life of their own! In an online daily paper, we read:

*The man **connected** his fist to the officer's face.* Once *connected*, we might imagine, the fist proceeds of its own accord to impart force to the officer's face, which results in a bruise. The fist is then taken into custody and denied bail.

In a paper of record, we find the headline:

*Missile at [Local] Cafe **Finds** Patrons Poised for World Cup.* A laser-guided missile saunters to the cafe, one is made to imagine, a toothpick hanging between its chapped lips, pushes through the batwing doors, and swiftly tips its wide-brimmed hat with thumb and forefinger.

A headline in the same paper, about a fatal airstrike, reminds us that beaches should learn to mind their own business:

*Rabbits **Drawn to** Beach and Into Center of Conflict.*

Elsewhere, we see actions attributed to an unknown actor, a vague collective, or an abstract concept—even though the responsible party is known with high confidence. A columnist for a paper of record shares, in a post:

*Our final wrap on **today's events, which left** 20 missing.*

In an official statement on a grant of clemency by an outgoing president, we read:

*When the convoy attempted to establish a blockade . . . the **situation turned** violent, **which resulted** in the unfortunate deaths and injuries of civilians.* The shots fired, and the four defense contractors holding the guns (and now being pardoned), are notably absent.

The headline for an online article about an airstrike that killed dozens reads:

*Badger Kingdom Said It Didn't Mean to Kill 42 Civilians. . . . It Attacked a Series of Underground Storage Units That **Caused Rabbits' Homes to Collapse**.*

This headline from a major cable news network (grammatically) transfers the action to the *recipient* . . .

*Beloved Woodland Bookshop **Becomes** a Casualty of Rabbit–Badger Conflict*

. . . without mentioning the laser-guided catapult or which of the two combatants launched it.

Similarly, a First Lady's personal friend recalls, with interesting remove:

*I'd **found myself** . . . planning the most divisive presidential inauguration in American history.* It's the worst, isn't it? When you're sitting around, minding your own business, and then you *find yourself* planning an inauguration.

ELEPHANT'S FOOT CONNECTED WITH MOUSE'S ROOF, WHICH CAUSED IT TO BECOME FLATTENED.

Examples like these crop up all the time:

Tower Housing [News Media] **Collapses** *after Missile Strike.*

Upper Rabbitton Teen Wounded by Badger Gunfire **Dies**.

Four Badger Guards Fired after a Rabbit **Dies** *in . . . Custody.*

Hiroshima marks 75th anniversary of **world's** *first atomic bombing.*

Violent protests **leave** *dozens dead.*

Rabbits zapped three badgers in an ambush last night; the event happened hours after six rabbits in a neighboring town **lost** *their lives.*

A journalist might choose such phrases more to help "take the edge off" unpleasant news than to intentionally dilute accountability. But let the reader beware media where the "slant" always goes one way—as in the last example, which attributes an action to rabbits in the first part, but not to badgers in the second part.

Misattributing quotes is a related tactic with a different outcome: Crediting one person's words to an entire group leaves less room for doubt. This can often be hard to spot. For instance, a line in *The Guardian* reads:

Witnesses *at the scene said that there was a "tremendous bang and then all hell broke loose."* Adding an *-es* transforms one person's account to a unanimous report.*

A CNN headline for what was deemed a bombshell article during a political contest reads:

Mr. Badger Told Rabbit in Private Meeting That a Rabbit Would Never Win, Sources Say. Specifically, four sources are cited. Later in the article, we find a line revealing that none of the four witnesses had firsthand knowledge of the meeting:

---

* Bill Bryson first identified this example in his *Dictionary of Troublesome Words*.

The description of that meeting is based on the accounts of four people: two people Rabbit spoke with directly soon after the encounter, and two people familiar with the meeting.

Thus might one eyewitness account, repeated to several, become a crowd of *sources*.

The passive voice is another popular way of disconnecting an action from whoever is committing it. The verb *to be* (in any tense) makes the recipient the subject of the sentence. No action verb? No actor required!

*The rabbit-badger war of 1974 led to the displacement of badger and rabbit populations in the city and its division. All badger residents of the northern part of the city **were expelled** by rabbit forces and the entire badger neighborhood was destroyed. Rabbit villages such as Purtown, Grumpytown, and Whiskertown **were depopulated**.*

Note how the *expulsion* is attributed to rabbits, despite the passive voice—but the *depopulation* is unattributed.

A police report about a bus driver who was beaten after asking three passengers to wear face masks is quoted:

*The victim pulled over the bus to escort the males off. As the victim was escorting the males off the bus one of the males pulled out a wooden bat and struck the victim several times, which caused the victim **to be injured**.*

An interviewer on BBC's *Newsnight* asks a minister if he knew that his security forces were so brutal. He replies:

*Mistakes **were made**. We don't tolerate human rights violations or torture.* The passive voice describes the bad thing; the active voice describes the good thing. We

An Illustrated Book of Loaded Language

end up with a shifting of blame, a weaseling out of any sense of responsibility. No one ever makes a mistake; mistakes are always made. No one ever commits a crime; crimes are always committed.

A carrot producer responds to an allegation of mistreating an employee with:

We have a responsibility to the rabbits mentioned and to our employees, and a fair investigation **will be conducted**. This interesting use of the passive voice leaves ambiguous *who* will conduct the investigation. We assume the company will take action by looking into the complaint—but in fact, they haven't committed to doing so.

Omitting detail. What's left *un*said is as much a part of any narrative as what's included. A government body may point to members of an underrepresented group in key positions, but leave out that *other* underrepresented groups are denied that same opportunity by law. An autocrat might have people "disappeared" from photographs and films to bring a narrative more in tune with the party line. Language that omits detail can do exactly the same thing.

Reporting on a political party's national convention, held to formally elect the party's presidential candidate, NBC News tweeted:

In one of the shortest speeches of the convention, the congresswoman **did not** *endorse the presumptive nominee Jim Bo*. While the statement is factually accurate, it omits a crucial detail: Organizers asked the congresswoman to endorse the runner-up candidate to acknowledge his efforts. Far from committing an act of rebellion (as the tweet attempts to insinuate), she was following protocol. The broadcaster later issued a clarifying note.

On the financial news website Barron's, we find the headline:

CEO Sold Shares Ahead of Stock Split. Later in the article, we read that the sale was announced well in advance, as is always the case with executives selling shares. The headline makes it seem like insider trading instead.

A piece in *The New York Times* opens with:

*In by far the largest protest yet here, **tens of thousands** of demonstrators packed the city's streets on Friday.* A paragraph later, we read that the crowd "appeared to be twice as large as one on Tuesday that drew about 100,000 people." While it's technically accurate to describe a crowd of 200,000 as made up of *tens of thousands* of demonstrators (as is saying it had *thousands* or *hundreds* or *tens* of protestors), that choice of words significantly downplays the magnitude and significance of such an event.

This brings to mind a related example: When asked how long it would take to resolve issues preventing people in the UK from getting tested for COVID-19, health secretary Matt Hancock replied, *a matter of weeks*. As Andy Zaltzman quips on an episode of *The News Quiz*, "It's been a matter of weeks since the Romans invaded. Just over a hundred thousand weeks, but still weeks."

More banally, a founder's professional profile reads:

Our company has signed multi-year client agreements with Google and Salesforce.com. On closer inspection, one finds that the company did nothing more than the ordinary task of paying for Google G Suite and Salesforce.com products, on behalf of its customers.

In corporate-speak, we see such statements as:

This quarter, we delivered several solutions that improved performance. Were they solutions to problems you created in the first place?

Last month we saw an uptick in customer emails asking for new features. Was it up from one to two?

In another example, a *Washington Post* headline reads:

This California City Defunded Its Police Force. Killings by Officers Soared. This headline seems to set up a tidy case against "defund the police" measures being considered in other cities. But the full article reveals that the city in question slashed its police budget (and force) because it ran out of money. It didn't reallocate any funds to social services—a key element of the other cities' proposals.

On a much more lighthearted note, comedian John Mulaney recalls a childhood episode in which he claimed to have brushed his teeth, only to be confronted with a dry toothbrush. His retort?

*I never specified that I brushed my teeth **today**.*

Waffling, with intention. Words such as *seem*, *allegedly*, and *probably* may be used to create more room for interpretation than the facts actually allow. In a book by a popular podcast host, we find this footnote:

*Many of my critics fault me for not engaging more directly with the academic literature. . . . My approach is to generally make an end run around many of the views and conceptual distinctions that make academic discussions of human values so inaccessible. While this is guaranteed to annoy a few people, the professional philosophers I've consulted **seem** to understand and support what I am doing.*

An Illustrated Book of Loaded Language

The professional philosophers are never named, and one is left wondering whether they do or don't support the author's approach. Suppose no supporters can be found: That *seem* gives the author room to claim an honest misunderstanding.

Something can be *alleged* (even if it isn't by any means libelous) to extend more "benefit of the doubt" to someone we like, or to make vague an otherwise clear series of events. For instance:

*Badger under fire for **allegedly** using anti-Rabbit slur during interview with radio host.* Did he or didn't he? If he didn't, it's not a story. If he did, it's not alleged.

A Wikipedia page reads (at time of writing):

*The rabbits' revolt was swiftly ended by the badger army's overwhelming military power. In this latest unrest, the badgers have been supported by four neighboring powers. The rabbits have **allegedly** been supported by two.* In this case, the badgers started a rumor that two widely disliked neighbors supported the rabbits. Thus, it's true that the support was *alleged*, but untrue that it existed. The article cements the false impression—history written by the victors in real time.

Probably and *might have* may be used to weaken an indisputable fact by introducing doubt:

*Spices became part of the national cuisine in the Badger Kingdom over time. Their popularity spread with the help of badgers in the eastern rabbit territories, who **probably** learned it from the local rabbits.*

They can also be used to imply wrongdoing without making an explicit accusation. In a TV interview, an activist recalls a meeting with an influential rival:

*Following my visit to his house, we agreed to abide by a set of terms. The ones I agreed to happened. The ones he agreed to **might not have** happened.*

Conflating confusable concepts. *Weather* and *climate*, often used interchangeably, offer a prime example of this strategy. A Sunday paper reads:

Closer to home, Austria is today seeing its earliest snowfall in history with 30 to 40 centimetres already predicted in the mountains. . . . Such dramatic falls in temperatures provide superficial evidence for those who doubt that the world is threatened by climate change. This glosses over scientists' stance that the effects of (global) climate change on (local) weather will include hotter *and* colder extremes. The wishy-washy phrasing of ***superficial** evidence **for those who doubt*** suggests the author is actually well aware.

Several months into the COVID-19 pandemic, the view that face masks can lead to oxygen deprivation seeped into some publications. A daily, albeit obscure, paper reads:

Studies reveal that wearing face masks can negatively affect the mind and body. The author goes on to cite a scientific finding that face masks reduce the oxygen level between the mask and one's mouth; the columnist then concludes that this reduces the oxygen level in the body, with some unspecified negative outcome. But this ignores other research showing that the body is able to compensate for such drops in oxygen intake.

Concealing with apparent precision. Specific "facts and figures" can lend an air of unquestionable truth—blinding us to the possibility that other, complicating data is left out. An article investigating bias in school admissions states:

At West Meadow Tech, beavers and hamsters make up only 15% and 3% of undergraduates, respectively, whereas 45% of area high school seniors who

An Illustrated Book of Loaded Language

meet WMT requirements are beavers and 4% are hamsters. Meeting the basic requirement for admission doesn't mean there weren't stronger candidates who filled the available spots.

In the run-up to the UK's European Union membership referendum in 2016, the prime minister stated:

Once we have settled our accounts, we will take back control of roughly **£350 million** *per week. It would be a fine thing, as many of us have pointed out, if* **a lot of** *that money went on the NHS.* The statement implies that around £350 million controlled by the EU would become available for the NHS. This ignores substantial incoming rebates from the EU, as well as ongoing commitments by the UK to other parties. The actual freed-up amount would be around £160 million per week.

An opening paragraph in a paper of record includes the following paraphrased line:

Rabbits with slingshots flung 800 carrots at badgers on Sunday, while badgers deafened 22 rabbits by screaming annoyingly through megaphones. An image is painted in the reader's mind: Relative to 800, 22 isn't that bad. Unmentioned, however, is that badgers have a sophisticated defense system that blocked an overwhelming majority of the carrots, and that badger injuries numbered 10 to the rabbits' 22.

When confronted with a number, ask yourself: What is the data source? Is it self-reported? Is it conflating something? Inferring something? Creating a cause-and-effect relationship without evidence? The answers will reveal whether the number follows the data, as it should, or whether it's the other way around. Percentages are particularly prone to misuse.

Apparent precision manifests as jargon as well—technical-sounding language, understood by a select group, that does anything but communicate with clarity.

The examples in this section show us how vagueness works to distance language from one of the very things it's meant to do—sincerely reflect reality. It's a good habit to read with skepticism—not necessarily suspicion, but at least skepticism—any line that (for instance) uses the passive voice, attributes actions to things, or drops a statistic. As we saw, a statistic might sound authoritative, but it can also be a mere red herring that helps an opinion pass as fact. The passive voice may signal that an actor is legitimately unknown, or it might *insinuate* that the actor is unknown.

A useful thought experiment, I find, is to turn contemporary headlines into anachronisms, which can further highlight their absurdity. A passive-voice headline from eighteenth-century America? How about:

*Low Cost of Cotton **Planted in** Southern States **Ensures** the South Continues to Be Debt-Free.*

2. LANGUAGE THAT CREATES SINISTER ASSOCIATIONS

> Once in every generation, without fail, there is
> an episode of hysteria about the barbarians.
>
> —*J. M. Coetzee*, Waiting for the Barbarians

"Once you label me, you negate me," as Kierkegaard is often quoted.* The brain is an association machine: Language with sinister associations encourages us to feel the same way about two possibly unrelated things by connecting them. What's the first thing that comes to mind when you read the word *Belfast* or *Beirut*?

It's for this very reason that writers extol the importance of travel, of being alone, of being far away: so we may fall into a silence that frees us from the heavily loaded assumptions and associations imposed by language.

Guilt by association. A quick way to predispose readers against someone is to evoke someone *else* they already dislike. A headline in a daily newspaper reads:

[Scary Organization's] *Executive Claims Son Died While en Route to a Wedding.* That same incident is reported by another paper with the more reasonable headline:

Man en Route to Wedding Shot Dead after Suspected Attack. The first headline elicits much less sympathy, thanks to the reference to Scary Organization. But did this person's life matter less because he had some indirect connection to this organization?

---

* The attribution may be apocryphal, but the point stands.

Similarly, in a grant of clemency by an outgoing president to four defense contractors accused of a heinous act, we read as follows:

*Prosecutors recently disclosed—more than 10 years after the incident—that the lead . . . investigator may have had ties to **insurgent groups** himself.* Nothing is said about the evidence in the case: The reader's attention is merely misdirected to the allegation that the investigator was partial because of ties he *may have had* to some unnamed evil group.

Elsewhere, a news video about an ambassador to the UK is titled:

Trump *Ambassador Investigated for Controversial Comments.* The qualifier at the start of this title implies a sort of ipso facto connection between who appointed the ambassador and the fact that he is being investigated. The viewer's feelings about Trump (whatever they are) are aroused before he or she even hits "play."

In a leading broadsheet, we find the headline:

Congresswoman *Condemns Death of Rabbit Child by Badger Forces*, and the article begins with a picture of the congresswoman and the lines:

*A teenage rabbit was killed on Friday . . . leading to international denunciation, including from congresswoman Jane Bo. Ms. Bo is a rabbit congresswoman who has faced accusations of being **anti-badger, a fierce critic of badgers**, and a supporter of economic movements aimed at pressuring the Badger Kingdom.*

Why is this particular politician given center stage in a story about an unarmed teenager being killed, one wonders?

Adding words, dropping words. Words or phrases that have negative connotations "built in" may be used to force an otherwise unspoken association.

Aid and abet is redundant, a tautology. Adding *abet*, though, suggests criminal intent. So, this word that adds no meaning may be introduced to insinuate malice. For instance:

[The Home Secretary] has all but declared war on [the strikers]. . . . She has also taken a swipe at those who **aid and abet** *them: human rights lawyers.*

Removing words also makes for effective sleight of hand. An opinion piece carries the headline:

Socialist *Politician Is Most Dangerous Major Party Presidential Contender in Rabbit Republic's History.* Here, the columnist conflates *socialist*, which evokes images of the Soviet Union, with *democratic socialist*—which ought to evoke images of Scandinavia—precisely in order to suggest that first, scarier connotation. A boogeyman would be objectively less scary if he came at you with biscuits in one hand and a princess cake in the other while repeating the phrase *Lagom är bäst.*

Metaphors and analogies. Other times, metaphors, analogies, and colorful imagery, either explicit or implied, do the dirty work. In the finance world, a bullish market may be described as *running hot*—and therefore due for a sell-off—by someone who stands to benefit from investors selling their positions. More insidiously, to make readers feel repulsion toward a group of people, a Sunday columnist writes:

Some of our towns are **festering sores, plagued by swarms** *of [them].*

Elsewhere, in a later-edited *New York Times* piece about large crowds gathering by the water during a heatwave, we find:

They **descended** *by the tens of thousands on Britain's southern beaches and* **jammed** *into city parks. They* **cavorted by the hundreds in swamps** . . .

That image brings to mind a piece from the 1970s. A TV reporter covering the 1977 disability rights sit-in at the Health, Education, and Welfare headquarters in San Francisco recounts:

*It all started this morning here at the old federal building at 50 Fulton when an incident took place outside. Immediately after that demonstration this morning, the handicapped started **invading** the building.*

A front-page headline from a few years earlier reads, in all caps no less:

CAPITOL IS INVADED, and follows with:

*A **band** of young men armed with **loaded** rifles, pistols and shotguns entered the Capitol Tuesday and **barged** into the assembly chamber during a debate.* The suggestion is obvious: That these people were all men, that they were breaking the law, and that they were foreign, alien beings, having traveled from a galaxy far, far away to *invade*, of all places, Sacramento.

Left unsaid is that the Black Panthers in question (men and women) were acting within the open-carry laws of the day, never pointed the guns at anyone, and left peacefully.

Loaded labels, slanted synonyms. Words whose political payloads are well understood can immediately shift how we feel about someone or something.

Radical. We call someone a *radical* to create associations with instability and absolutist, impractical, dangerous, idealist thinking. For that reason, a person's mere existence may be cause for being called a radical. Time, strangely enough, has a way of bringing yesterday's "radicals" into the fold of acceptability, and even reverence.

Urban. Some labels are used as "dog whistles," a phenomenon one finds in political rhetoric. A speaker will use coded words or phrases, meant to be understood one way by like-minded listeners, while appearing benign to everybody else. This gives the speaker plausible deniability if accused of bigotry toward a group they didn't *expressly* name. In US politics, *urban* might be used to signify *minorities*, Black people especially, and *suburban* might be used to exclude them. As in this statement by a former politician:

I am happy to inform all of the people living their Suburban Lifestyle Dream that you will no longer be bothered or financially hurt by having low-income housing built in your neighborhood.

Woke. Kids these days! A *Wall Street Journal* subheading about Trader Joe's reads: *The grocer takes **woke** orders on its brands from a 17-year-old*. One little word, often derided, is all it takes to insinuate that young people don't have the capacity to offer good advice.

Regime. We might call a government or a specific administration a *regime* if we don't like it. When two groups are vying for political power, it's common to see headlines from each side referring to itself as a *government* and to the other as a *regime*: *Sturgeon General Says Rabbit **Administration** Will Be "Transparent and Honest" on COVID Unlike Badger **Regime***.

Related, a headline about lawmakers organizing to make a political push reads: *Badgers **Plot** Head of Government's Removal after Deadly Riots*. *Plotting* suggests a clandestine act rather than a banal, expected one.

Enemy combatant. We might call someone an *enemy combatant* or a *guerrilla fighter* or an *insurgent* or an *agitator* or a *rebel* or a *militia fighter*—or, on the flip side, a member of the *resistance* or a *commando*—based on whether or not that person's interests match ours.

An Illustrated Book of Loaded Language

Banana republics. Repeated often enough, loaded labels become self-reinforcing. In a TV debate about the international community's position on a contentious conflict, a guest—a notable historian, no less—states:

*The international community, except for some **banana republics** in Africa, did not vote in favor of those resolutions.* It's later revealed that the statement is factually inaccurate. But even so, the guest's insinuation is that so-called *banana republics* (which originally referred to economic exploitation) can't ever vote their conscience on moral motions.

MERS, Spanish flu. Associating dangerous diseases with certain geographic locations or populations can imply that the diseases are *inherent* in those locations or populations. *MERS* (Middle East Respiratory Syndrome) is a recent example. The *Spanish flu*, which in all likelihood didn't originate in Spain, is a more distant one.

Today, scientific guidance is against naming diseases after characteristics like geography, principally to avoid unintended backlash—*Alpha variant* is better than *UK variant*. Nearly a third of Asian Americans say they've experienced some form of discrimination since the COVID-19 pandemic.

Hyperbole. We're constantly reading headlines about people *slamming* or being slammed, *blasting* or being blasted, *destroying* or being destroyed. These embellishments normalize a charged, polarized political culture; they make it easy for opportunists and populists to gain a foothold in the mainstream. Desperate times call for desperate measures! More generally, these phrases grab (and redirect?) our attention (just like *Breaking News* and *Key Race Alert*, to name two of several CNN favorites).

An Illustrated Book of Loaded Language

A quick rundown of some examples:

*VP Candidate **Slams** Badger Administration.*

*Jim Acosta **Blasted** for Taking Kayleigh McEnany out of Context in Viral Tweet.*

*Furious Senator **Lashes Out** at Former Colleagues.*

And again:

*A Geopolitical **Earthquake Just Hit** [the Region].* Miraculously, no structural damage was reported.

*The former First Lady **flayed, sliced, and diced** the current president in her speech.* No word yet on who mopped up all the blood.

*Renters Break Leases and **Flee** City.* You'd think they were scrambling to board the last helicopter out of Vietnam, as Brian Regan might say.

*Natural . . . threats seem to **multiply by the hour**.* Yet somehow we've lived to read this.

*The **Battle** for the Country Begins.* Civil war? Nope, a senatorial runoff election.

*Kanye West Gets **Thrown Off** the Ballot in Wisconsin.* Poor Kanye. It's just not right.

*Zuckerberg **Dumped on** by Facebook Employees Over Handling of Militia Groups.* Oh dear. That can't be pleasant.

This kind of language projects the world as a wild, tough, rough place—one that only a lone hero on saddleback can sort out. A newspaper's editorial board writes:

*In the midst of **unrelenting chaos**, [the candidate] is offering an anxious, exhausted nation **something beyond** policy or ideology.* As one commentator points out, policy and ideology are precisely what constituents expect from their politicians. Unless the *something beyond* is actually divine or metaphysical—even if it's simply character and values, which the paper is likely referring to—it had better manifest as policy. Otherwise it's not of much use.

Taking cues from the Marvel universe, a subheadline reads:

If Badger wins [the election], it will be seen as the moment when the **destiny of a mammal and his nation converged**.

All in all, negative associations are easy to form, often through proximity—two words appearing close to one another—and through incessant repetition. Of course, hyperbole can be rewritten with a focus on precision instead. For instance:

Kanye West ~~Gets Thrown Off the Ballot in Wisconsin~~ Is Disqualified for

VP Candidate ~~Slams~~ Criticizes *Badger Administration.* Missing Deadline.

Examples of guilt by association can be made more factual by asking whether the association adds anything substantive, or whether it betrays bias on our part:

~~Trump~~ US *Ambassador Investigated for Controversial Comments.*

~~Congresswoman Condemns Death of~~ Rabbit Child by Badger Forces.

And extra words are easily removed: Is Killed

[The Home Secretary] has all but declared war on [the strikers] . . . she has also taken a swipe at those who aid ~~and abet~~ them: human rights lawyers.

Making or implying a sinister association is one way of shifting a narrative. Next, we'll consider the opposite approach: drawing associations that make a narrative more positive, or more palatable, than the facts on the ground.

3. LANGUAGE THAT CREATES FEEL-GOOD ASSOCIATIONS

A magazine wanting you to renew your subscription will call out the intelligence, wit, style, and humor that you would be missing out on if you don't, as *The New Yorker* does. Another magazine will paint you a picture of that one person at a dinner party who always has something interesting to say. You can be that person, you're told—all you need to do is renew your subscription. It might not sit right; you sense that the language is loaded; but you feel special all the same.

A notable example that went on to save a company from doom is De Beers' campaign in the 1940s. It aimed to suggest diamonds had some intrinsic value with the lines: *How can you make two months' salary last forever? The Diamond Engagement Ring. A Diamond Is Forever.* Between 1940 and 1990, the percentage of first-time brides who received diamond engagement rings in the US went up from 10 to 80 percent.

Often, feel-good associations aim to entice us to do something we usually wouldn't. Other times, they're more sinister: Euphemisms, for instance, can help us disassociate from a repellant action, thereby removing any residual sense of guilt. And one positive quality thrown into the middle of a description might convince us that someone isn't so bad after all. An article on an ABC affiliate's website describes a man who stormed the US Capitol in January 2021:

[Jack], **who addressed the judge as "ma'am" and "your honor,"** *also faces charges of stealing public property and violent entry and disorderly conduct on Capitol grounds.* One is left wondering how that detail adds anything substantive to the story.

Here are some other examples.

All-natural adjectives. Positive-sounding words help convince us to buy things and—crucially—to accept ideas that wouldn't be palatable otherwise. In one of his live acts, George Carlin rattles off a catalog of feel-good phrases from advertising: "Sometime during my life, *toilet* paper became *bathroom tissue!*" William Lutz covers quite a few examples as well—plenty from the twentieth century—in his essay and book on doublespeak.

Free implies low-risk, zero-loss. TurboTax's online marketing copy suggests their product is free not once, but multiple times:

*Free Guaranteed. Easily and accurately file your simple tax returns for **FREE**.* Their product is anything but *free:* Over 90 percent of filers who qualify for the free product end up paying for it.

Related, one might argue that NAFTA (the North American *Free Trade* Agreement) is not so much about free trade as it is about ensuring multinational corporations can protect their investments in new markets, and thus maximize profit. Duncan Green writes that the bulk of the agreement "concerns investment rather than trade, and in almost every case, it concerns Mexico, rather than the United States or Canada. NAFTA . . . binds Mexico into strict new patent rules for pharmaceuticals and computer software and prevents Mexico from trying to delay or obstruct the repatriation of profits by transnational companies."

Sustainable. Some manufacturers refer to their electric cars as *sustainable*, even though not everything about them is. The batteries, for instance, require mining the earth for rare elements. Half of the world's cobalt is used in batteries, and that number is expected only to increase in the decades to come. As space tourism takes shape and companies compete for future bookings, this word is likely to be co-opted there, too.

An Illustrated Book of Loaded Language

ALL ABOARD FOR tHE ANNUAL RABBIt MEEt!

Natural. The dessert, snack, and beverage aisles at a grocery store are chock-full of high-calorie, high-sugar foods, some containing—supposedly—*natural flavors*. As far as the FDA is concerned, *natural* is not well defined: Class A drugs come from nature, as do quack medicines. But *natural* makes us feel good, because it implies *not artificial*, which implies *from the earth*, which implies *good for you*.

Other vague terms marketers use for the same purpose include: *plant-based, healthy, fat-free* (but full of sugar?), *low-cholesterol, up to* (as in ***up to*** *60 percent off*), *new and improved, best, exclusive, guaranteed, on sale, authentic, tested, certified, limited-edition, bestselling*, and many others. Asking "relative to what?" or "with what tradeoff?" is often illuminating.

Scientific. A scientific tone can disguise beliefs or opinions as fact. Consider *think tanks*, which evoke an image of sophistication and objective inquiry. In reality, the more influential think tanks are often well-funded groups of like-minded individuals who trade in intellectual-sounding language that justifies hard-set preconceptions.

Democratic. A system of government, either sanctimoniously or as a smokescreen, might call itself *democratic* or make a similarly grand claim about how it affords representation. The irony of an autocracy calling itself a democracy might seem blazingly obvious, but repeated often enough and in the right geopolitical climate, this can in fact have the desired propagandistic effect.

As Orwell writes, "In the case of a word like *democracy*, not only is there no agreed definition, but the attempt to make one is resisted from all sides. It is almost universally felt that when we call a country democratic we are praising it: Consequently the defenders of every kind of regime claim that it is a democracy."

An Illustrated Book of Loaded Language

Patriotic. A bill that curtails personal freedoms and civil liberties has an easier chance of passing into law if it's called something like *The Flag-Waver Act* or *The Freedom Act*.

Easy-to-swallow euphemisms.[*] Euphemisms make us feel better about something by glossing over the worst parts. Even phrases that still sound a bit negative can serve this feel-good function.

Economically disadvantaged sounds better than *economically exploited*. Granted, economic disparity isn't always due to exploitation—but in the context of developed and developing nations, it often can be. India's share of the world economy tanked from 24 to 4 percent over a century and a half of exploitation, and the question of how that happened doesn't come up nearly as often as it should.

Urban renewal sounds like a neighborhood is getting better (albeit at the cost of its former residents, of course). "*Better* never means better for everyone," as The Commander tells Offred in *The Handmaid's Tale*.

Quantitative easing sounds more responsible than *printing free money to prop up the stock market*. (Perhaps in time for an election?) It's true that easing may bring short-term economic growth by reducing the cost of borrowing money, but the longer-term risk of inflation is often left unmentioned, as in:

The Fed should get rid of quantitative tightening. . . . You would see a rocket ship.

Imposing sanctions on a country implies that they must have done something horrendous, worthy of severe punishment. In some cases, it's a more useful,

[*] From the Greek *eu-* (meaning "well") and *phēmē* (meaning "speech")

sanctimonious term for applying *unilateral economic measures as a means of political and economic coercion*, as a UN resolution puts it.

Military and related contexts are particularly rife with these roundabout catchphrases:

Ministry of Defense is more respectable than *Ministry of War*. It implies we're reacting to aggression whenever we engage in combat. In principle, the name change is perfectly reasonable in our post–World War II era, but it doesn't always hold up on examination. It's a bit hard to rationalize a Badger bomber flying over Rabbit country *in a defensive move* when one looks at a map and sees the two nations 7,000 miles apart. In the same vein, defense contractors are in the business of *defending*, forces like the Peninsula Shield are in the business of *shielding*, and national security laws are in the business of *securing*.

Rubber bullets, much like **sponge grenades**, sound softer, kinder, gentler, and more civilized than steel bullets. The term hides the fact that many rubber bullets contain a metal core. Rubber bullets blind, maim, and even kill—yet, when we read *rubber bullets*, we think *nonlethal* or *less lethal weapons*. A man of the cloth, defending an army's use of such bullets (perhaps taken in by their bouncy-sounding name), goes so far as to take them as evidence of good intentions:

*You see in that word "rubber bullets" the tension of **trying to carry out a [moral] vision** in the real world.*

Similarly, **excited delirium** sounds more organic than *death by Taser*—a syndrome pushed into the mainstream, coincidentally, by the Taser company Axon, via its catalog of self-funded studies and network of experts, researchers, and consultants.

Anti-rabbit fighter. In a world where it's a given that rabbits are the enemy, calling someone an *anti-rabbit fighter* lends them legitimacy right off the bat. They're anti-rabbit, we're anti-rabbit; so naturally, we must both be righteous. This selective yardstick conflates which side you're on with whether your actions are morally permissible.

Defining morality based on who happens to be on the other side is why, as Gabor Maté puts it, our media praises a protestor throwing stones at government forces in, say, Hong Kong, but demonizes the exact same act committed in some other part of the world.

Civil unrest. An external power waging war on a sovereign state may describe the resulting conflict as a *civil war*, or as *civil unrest*, rather than a *conquest* that's opposed by a *liberation movement*. *Civil unrest* presumes some degree of parity between two sides and eliminates the need for nuance. Calling it a *liberation movement*, on the other hand, reveals the truth about a people rising up for a primal reason, usually at great personal cost.

Moving tactically makes it easier to justify an overreaction:
*The sniper, sensing impending danger, fatally shot the farmer. The farmer was described as **moving tactically**.* And saying a **military-aged male** was targeted is somehow more forgivable than saying a *bystanding teenager* was targeted.

Cleansing, purging. *Cleansing* leaves you with a cleaner kitchen counter. Thus, public squares are *cleansed* of sit-in students, streets are *cleansed* of demonstrators, towns and cities are *cleansed* of undesirable populations. *Purging* suggests the elimination of something harmful or toxic. *Purging* institutions and government agencies sounds better than saying who was forcibly removed, for what reason, and what terrible fate befell them.

Pacification suggests bringing something back to its natural state. Its definition reveals an eerie dual meaning:

> a) the act or process of pacifying (to restore to a tranquil state)
>
> b) the act of forcibly suppressing or eliminating a population considered to be hostile.

A headline in *The Guardian* reads:

Bears Vow Not to Stop Attacks Until There Is **"Complete Quiet."** *Quiet*, as in a state in which the enemy is utterly and mortally crushed.

And again:

Acts sound better than *atrocities* when referring to massacres of civilians.

Administrative detention sounds better than *incarceration without trial*.

Collateral damage sounds better than *civilian deaths*.

Community sounds more agreeable than *settlement*.

Controlled or **disputed** sounds more agreeable than *occupied*.

Enhanced interrogation sounds better than good old *torture*.

Eviction sounds better than *forced expulsion* or *ethnic cleansing*.

Kinetic military action sounds better than *dropping bombs*.

Military target sounds better than *families of military targets*.

Ordnance sounds better than *weapons*.

Population transfer and **depopulation**, unlike *forced migration*, don't bring any image to mind of the immense human cost involved.

Private military company sounds better than *mercenary*.

Reeducation camp sounds less sinister than *internment* or *concentration camp*.

Security fence sounds more agreeable than *border wall*.

Tearing down evokes memories of the Berlin Wall—it's much easier on the eyes and ears than *demolish*, *bulldoze*, or *destroy*.

It's out of our hands. Attributing rejection or dysfunction to *things*, or to people with less power than the actual decisionmakers, makes them easier to take.

A wave of layoffs seems like an inevitability, a force of nature—something that was out of the CEO's power. Much like a *cycle of violence* sounds somehow self-perpetuating without any human input.

Externalities is a handy catch-all euphemism for redirecting blame (to nowhere), as in: The project is two years behind schedule not because the mayor didn't step up, but because of *externalities*.

Carbon footprints suggest that the everyday activities of ordinary people are major contributors to global warming. This term—popularized by British Petroleum with catchy blurbs like *It's time to go on a low-carbon diet*—ingeniously shifts responsibility away from fossil-fuel companies.

Similarly, your bank didn't reject you; your own *credit score* disqualified you. Facebook or Instagram didn't take your post down; it fell short of *community standards*. (Never mind that it complied with Facebook's terms of use.) *Software glitches* often take the blame when inconvenient content is deleted on social media websites.

Algorithms, just like any kind of automation, can also conceal built-in bias. As might statements like *Let's see what **the data** tells us*. If you're not careful, the data will tell you anything you want it to.

It's all up to you. An authority wishing to impose limits on what's acceptable free speech and what's not may put a few "well-behaved" dissenters on a pedestal, as if to say to the rest, "This is what you're missing out on by not falling in line." The speed, direction, and type of progress can then be laid at the feet of these seemingly empowered individuals. In a radio debate between a fringe civil-rights proponent and an expert on civil-rights movements, we hear the following exchange about the race problem in America:

Activist: "Our current community leaders are not succeeding in getting anything done for our people, sir. They're complacent in our disenfranchisement."

Expert: "I believe the word you're looking for is *responsible*. They're responsible."

It's for the greater good. Feel-good turns of phrase also crop up to obscure *who profits*. Referring to *children* or other helpless beings is one way to sound selfless while advocating for something you want:

This new policy will help us ensure a better world for our children. This can also be useful as a headfake, in order to get a bill passed into law, for instance. A recent bill that aims to prevent companies from using end-to-end encryption goes by the name *Eliminating Abusive and Rampant Neglect of Interactive Technologies Act of 2020*, and promises to protect children against online abusers. Of course, if passed, it will do much more than that, by effectively giving government agencies a backdoor into encrypted communication channels.

Human capital refers to the valuable knowledge we transfer between cultures and across generations. In an interview, Peter Robinson whitewashes the immense suffering and looting that are part and parcel of colonialism, reflecting nostalgically on Empire:

*People who have looked at the British colonies, on balance [find] it's **a transfer of human capital**. They're not impoverishing the people . . . on the contrary.*

Prepositions and possessives can succinctly swap these roles. Robert Clive going by *Clive **of** India* suggests that he belonged to India, when in fact, as one Indian MP states, it was India that belonged to him. The royal title *Custodian **of** the Three Big Islands* suggests a monarch is in service to a set of prosperous cities, when in reality it's the other way around.

It's only reasonable. When we don't want to deal with our real antagonists because that requires too much effort or empathy, we often deem a subset of them *moderates*. That token group is then made the legitimate face of the one we are unwilling or unable to deal with.

A columnist, well-versed in false dilemmas, writes:

*Those in the **pro-us, pro-moderate** camp benefit the most from this development and those in the **radical, anti-us** camp will become more isolated and will be left behind.*

Similarly, when we don't want to take action (but don't want to appear negligent) we'll refer something *for further consideration*. This phrase creates the sense that we're in fact showing caution by not getting anything done. It shows up often in stagnating organizations.

A funny aside—in 1944, the Office of Strategic Services (the CIA's predecessor) published the *Simple Sabotage Field Manual*. Under "General interference with organizations and production," it includes, "When possible, refer all matters to committees, for 'further study and consideration.' Attempt to make the committees as large as possible—never less than five."

The passage of time has a way of revealing euphemisms and other such feel-good language for what they are. When a leader takes a nation to war, and pays an enormous price for winning it, it's very hard for them to not project it as a victory. Otherwise, what was it all for? But from the vantage point of later generations, *victory* might well turn into *massacre*, and *liberation* might well turn into *exploitation*. It's ironic how hard it can be to remain objective to something the closer you get to it. Perhaps that's where the idiom "The spectator sees more of the game" comes from.

4. LANGUAGE THAT PRESUPPOSES

> We make to ourselves pictures of facts.
>
> —*Ludwig Wittgenstein*

We "presuppose" when we take something as a given—as fact. But undeniable, objective facts can end up being interpreted through the lens of those who wield the greatest influence. The resulting "pictures of facts" get disseminated to everybody as though they *were* facts—becoming what Nietzsche calls a "mobile army of metaphors, metonyms, and anthropomorphisms . . . which have been enhanced, transposed, and embellished poetically and rhetorically, and which after long use seem firm, canonical, and obligatory to a people."

Stereotypes and bias, in particular, become entrenched through this type of loaded language, as we'll see.

Irrelevant adjectives. Highlighting an incidental quality helps push a narrative that may not be in accordance with reality. For instance:

*Clashes with **brown-haired** rabbits left three badgers injured.* Having brown hair adds no useful context. Repeated often, it may eventually give the impression that it somehow does—especially if offenders with *other* hair colors are described simply as *rabbits*.

On one episode of a clinical psychologist's CBS talk show, the host repeatedly and gratuitously refers to one of his guests as a *brown-haired* rabbit, to no objectively useful end. Since this guest was being castigated as if some sort of monster, the repetition clearly aimed to associate his actions with the irrelevant quality of having brown hair.

We see the same dynamic at work when, in times of conflict, a hospital is called a *rabbit-run hospital* or a school is called a *rabbit-run school*.

"Inherent" versus acquired qualities. A rabbit who sets fire to public property might be called an *arsonist*—as if born that way—while a badger who commits the same act might be referred to as exhibiting *arsonist-like tactics*. Wherever did he learn to do that?

Following an attack on a federal building that led to casualties and property damage and drew widespread condemnation, a badger journalist shared:

*Today reminded me of my time reporting from the Rabbit Kingdom. It felt like we were in some **third world** country. **This is not us. This is not who we are.*** The same sentiment was repeated by a senator the very next morning. One wonders how the rabbits listening to this kind of reality-defying rhetoric must have reacted.

When people are taking to the streets, an official statement might read:

*Two protests have broken out in the city's north and south sides. Angry rioters have taken to the streets down south, while **the good people** up north have camped in front of City Hall.*

Not too long ago, a rabbit entered a grocery store owned by badgers and nibbled on all their carrots. The next morning, a headline read:

*Badger Town Hit by Another Murderous **Rabbit** Attack, a Dozen Carrots Perish.* One day later, a badger was caught attempting to do the same thing in Whiskertown— rabbit land. That headline read:

*Attacker in Whiskertown Is **Anti-Carrot Extremist***. Granted, *extremist* is an absolutely fair descriptor for someone who commits an uncivilized act like this one. But the second headline is much more coy about the badger's identity than the first one is about the rabbit's. Further coverage of the badger attack reads:

*The attack took place **near a psychiatric hospital**, but there is no evidence to suggest the offender was a patient at the hospital.* The psychiatric hospital is a strange item to have casually thrown into the mix. A reader wouldn't be faulted for assuming that the badger was not of sound mind—which is to say, not his true, pure, badger self.

Identity passed as *prima facie* evidence. Once negative traits are considered innate to a particular group, membership in that group may be held up as sufficient "proof" of guilt, inferiority, or intent—no actual evidence required. An influential podcaster opines:

When we look at the conflict between badgers and rabbits, there is every reason to believe that if badgers had all the power in the world, they would use it to build a prosperous kingdom. And if that imbalance were reversed, rabbits would use it to drive all the badgers out of the forest.

In a daily YouTube show, a physician muses:

*Now, we can't entirely be sure about the accuracy of the data about active cases coming to us from **that country**; they may well be underestimates, in fact, I'm sure they are.* No evidence is offered for why it's more probable than not that the data coming from that country is inaccurate.

SEEING YOUNG RABBITS EXCITED ABOUT OUR SPACE LAUNCH WARMED MY HEART. THAT'S ONE LESS RABBIT ON A CORNER SOMEWHERE, WAITING FOR NIGHTFALL TO GO RAID A CARROT PATCH.

We find this kind of reasoning elsewhere, too: How we talk about a vaccine produced by a country can depend on which country it is, and if we like it or not. When someone alleged to be a spy is caught on foreign soil, whether that person is presumed guilty often depends on where they're from and where they've been arrested.

In a 2018 interview with a professor, we hear:

*The fact remains that **every rabbit** walking around Mount Royal Park wearing a baseball hat is making a political statement.* Not every cultural identifier is meant as an affront or statement to the world at large, professor.

Elsewhere, on the internet, beneath a polemic berating an author for being disingenuous, a commentor asserts confidently: *This man is funded by the Hokey Pokey brothers.*

"Is he actually funded by them in any way?" responds another, drawing the reply:

*He certainly **feels like exactly the kind of ghoul** they would throw money at.*

More perniciously, we can go so far as to define who is good and who is evil by identity alone. In the writings of a foreign minister, we find:

*The prime minister and I underscored the importance of countering the Rabbit Kingdom's **malign influence** and threats to the region. I thanked him for his partnership.* But minister, one feels compelled to point out, you yourself spend much of your time in that same region in hopes of spreading your influence. Not that it has any bearing on whether the Rabbit Kingdom's influence is good or evil, but the clear presupposition is that *our* actions are categorically good, and the same actions, by somebody we don't like, aren't.

Modern, civilized. Writing can adopt the perspective that other people can't be *modern*, often a euphemism for *civilized*, unless they dress like us, eat like us, speak like us, think like us, and so on. Thus, we make ourselves the yardstick for who is civilized, then dismiss other cultures as backward and inferior—or perhaps as *third world* countries, as we saw a moment ago.

That is, unless they have something we really like, in which case we "civilize" it by claiming it as our own:

Coffee . . . the favorite beverage of the **civilized** *world.*

Rodgers and Hammerstein grapple with the self-centeredness of this approach, even while arguably succumbing to it at times, in their musical *The King and I.* As the King of Siam's wives are preparing to meet, and hopefully impress, visiting Western dignitaries, they wonder aloud why they must adopt the clear mistakes of their would-be civilizers: cumbersome hoop skirts and leather shoes that pinch. They can only conclude (as the song title puts it): "Western People Funny."

Interestingly this particular song is often cut from productions.

Defining normal. In a recent work of fiction, we find the following two lines:

How cruel that they punished you **for something you cannot change**.

We love you **no matter what**. Both imply that there is, in fact, something wrong with the person in question. (Even if that person *could* change themselves, why would they if nothing is wrong?) As James Baldwin writes in an essay, "Language, incontestably, reveals the speaker. Language, also, far more dubiously, is meant to define the other."

Related, we sometimes hear from well-meaning souls the phrase:

*Everyone should feel comfortable being their **authentic self**.* This phrase, while popular, presupposes that the cost of being authentic is the same for everyone. The truth of the matter is that not everyone can reveal themselves without paying a social price, which in some cases is a price too high to pay.

But. This conjunction is sometimes cavalierly squeezed between a grandiose claim and a fleeting admission of why, just maybe, that claim might not be supported. *But* is thus a helpful flag for presupposition masquerading as fact. For instance:

*You just might end up richer [if you read a book for an hour before bed]. Correlation is definitely not causation here, **but** the same survey found bedtime readers make an average of $3,705 more annually.*

In 1850, the anatomist Robert Knox wrote:

I feel disposed to think there must be a physical and, consequently, a psychological inferiority [between rabbits and badgers] generally. He goes on for the rest of the page to describe the differences, ending with:

***but** I speak from extremely limited experience.* As the narrator of the four-part documentary series *Exterminate All the Brutes* quips after reading that line, the anatomist had at the time done an autopsy on a single rabbit, "which somehow does demonstrate the limitations of his experiments." I suppose it does.

Foregone conclusions. Self-assured phrases and preambles can be used to "sell" us presuppositions about the world as fact, without evidence. They suggest that whatever follows or precedes them is unarguable, or universally applicable—when in fact it may well be opinion, or even an outright boast:

An Illustrated Book of Loaded Language

In the final analysis, the goal of life is to be happy. (In *whose* final analysis?)

As we all know, if you want to be happy, quit your day job and follow your passion.

As it turns out, spell-checking in software is a solved problem.

*You can't believe that, **surely**.* (Common in British English.)

*Some people browsing my work have called it the ultimate map of maps, **right**.* (Common in Silicon Valley English.)

*Books never go back before the eighteenth century to explain the origins of data visualization, **right**.*

Similar phrases include: *the fact of the matter is, it is generally assumed, it therefore follows, so, obviously, naturally, rather, at the end of the day,* and *when all's said and done.*

Telling others how the world is or ought to be—without evidence—betrays our own biases, implicit and conscious, about others. Our words reveal us, more than they do others. To realize how contemptuous this can appear, imagine if a badger were to narrate a rabbit's every move, in the style of a David Attenborough nature documentary (much like Gustave Flaubert did as he walked the streets of Cairo): "And here. We find a rabbit. We shall call him Bob. Bob walks up to a bush. Bob must be starving . . ."

5. LANGUAGE THAT FEIGNS OBJECTIVITY WITH APPARENT NEUTRALITY

To be objective is a good thing; it means to set aside any bias and consider the facts. To be neutral is slightly different; it means not taking a side in an argument. One of the hardest things to spot is language that *sounds* objective (because it's neutral) but is actually *sub*jective (influenced by opinion). This is often a telltale sign that someone's words cannot be taken at face value. Other times, the appeal to objectivity is misplaced altogether: Not every argument has two equally logical and legitimate sides.

False equivalence. Language can give equal weight to things that are disproportionate, because the writer wants either to remain noncommittal or to obscure an otherwise self-evident truth. Consider:

Yesterday's **violence left** *12 rabbits with lost limbs and one badger with slight shoulder pain; the UN secretary general urged* **both sides** *to show restraint.* Language like this does away with all detail. We are left with a static view of an event's aftermath; we are compelled to sympathize with its effects rather than seek any insight into its cause.

A newspaper of note reads:

The nation cannot afford to say "amen" to **either** *form of extremism, rabbit or badger.* As an abstract statement of fact, this sentiment is perfectly reasonable. But within the context of that particular day in history, on which the violence had been clearly one-sided, the line is heavily loaded.

LOCAL FISH DESCRIBE THE POND AS HALF EMPTY,
WHILE NEIGHBORING CRANES SEE IT AS HALF FULL.
THE DEBATE CONTINUES.

Some *say face masks are effective in stopping the spread of the virus;* **others** *are not so sure.* The line, which showed up more often that it should have near the start of the pandemic, is disingenuous; it removes all nuance of which view is more or less likely by omitting the identities of the two (one supposes, equally qualified?) groups.

The senator, though he calls himself an independent, is **to others** *a raging socialist.* All it takes for this line to be factually true is for one person to hold each view. But the questions remain whether either view is in accordance with reality, and whether any split in how the senator is perceived is indeed proportional.

As *The Guardian*'s Bob Garfield points out, this *Washington Post* op-ed attempts to offer a balanced narrative of the 2013 US government shutdown, but ends up mischaracterizing the lead-up to it:

Ultimately, the grown-ups in the room will have to do their jobs, which in a democracy with divided government means compromising for the common good. . . . **Both sides are inordinately concerned** *with making sure that, if catastrophe comes, the other side takes the political hit.* The shutdown wasn't due to a split between left and right, but rather to a faction of the Republican party using the shutdown (unsuccessfully) as a way to pressure the senate into repealing the Affordable Care Act.

Even the blazingly obvious can be turned into a two-sided issue. In response to the kidnapping of a journalist by a person of influence, an official statement from a world power reads:

*Our intelligence agencies continue to assess all information, but it could very well be that [the person in question] had knowledge of this tragic event—***maybe he did and maybe he didn't***!* A tautology that, in so many words, says nothing whatsoever.

It takes two to tango. Words like *war* and *clash* evoke two matched combatants equally intent on fighting. They are sometimes *mis*used to falsely give that impression. A tweet by an influential koala reads:

My country is **at war**. *My heart breaks.* On inspection, one finds the conflict in question doesn't involve two countries, but rather Koalaland and a group of kangaroos living in an enclave. Koalaland has a ground force, a navy, an air force, sophisticated guidance technology, and all the other things wealthy, well-equipped countries have; the other belligerent has none of those things. The nonexistent symmetry implied by the word *war* is often used to justify the resulting losses of life and property—largely on the kangaroo side.

A day after tensions escalated in a neighborhood, due to marauding badgers roaming the streets, calling for all rabbits to be expelled, a major news outlet's headline read:

More Than 100 Animals Injured in Last Night's **Clashes**.

Similarly, a *Reuters* headline reads:

Rabbits, Badgers **Clash** *Downtown, Scores Injured.* No distinction is made between rabbits and badgers—either as instigators, or in numbers among the injured.

A headline in a newspaper of record reads:

Badgers Say That Rabbits Use Baby Rabbits as Shields, Reviving **Debate**. Per that newspaper, a fitting way to cover a situation in which hundreds of unarmed rabbits become casualties at the hands of badgers is as a *debate*.

Prevaricating. To prevaricate is to use wishy-washy language that avoids taking a firm stance—either cynically or as a cop-out. The resulting tone often seems "neutral" until you consider which assertions are waffled, and to whose benefit or detriment. For instance:

*We caught up with a man who **some people are calling** racist after he yelled at a neighbor.* Was he or wasn't he yelling racist sentiments? If he wasn't, one might ask, then aren't you slandering him? If he was, then why the insincere language?

***Apparent** badger extremist attack in rabbit neighborhood comes amid continued tensions in capital and leaves three cars torched.* Was the attacker a badger or wasn't he? This same article pinned a tit-for-tat attack on a rabbit, without waffling.

*This is a video showing people toppling a statue of Jim Bo. He wrote our national anthem and was also **known to have been** a tax evader.* Was he or wasn't he?

*Today we bring you a video that **seems to have been** vertically taken.* Was it or wasn't it?

*Video **appears to** show Capitol Hill police officer taking selfie with rioter.* Does it or doesn't it?

*Most of the injuries were to the face and eyes and **appeared to be** caused by rubber bullets.* It's fairly straightforward to tell if an injury was caused by a rubber bullet.

*While the first author's clarification appeased some fans, it **appears to have** irked the second author. Some social media users have also **speculated that** the two unfollowed each other on Twitter.* Did they or didn't they? It would have been easy to confirm that before running the story.

It's complicated. Language sometimes tries to convince the reader that a situation is so complicated and messy, it's impossible to take a moral or factual stance on it. We find this mindset in some intellectual realms as well, where objective truth is deemed unknowable and the world cast as a set of conflicting, equally legitimate narratives.

IT'S COMPLICATED.

"Mr. Badger, sir, what do you think of the fact that badgers control the entire supply of carrots and sell them to rabbits at extortionate prices?"

Well, **it's complicated**. *An entanglement, as they say in Hollywood.*

In an interview, a secretary of defense shared his thoughts on an explosion that led to thousands of casualties. Contrary to consensus in the international and intelligence communities, this secretary had previously assigned malice to what evidence suggests was an accident due to negligence:

We thought it might have been an attack, it could have been an armed shipment, a bomb-making facility, **who knows**? *Yesterday I commented that it was looking like an accident.*

After an assault on the US Capitol by an identifiable group of people, a congressman comments:

I also think everybody across this country has some responsibility.

A headline in a paper of record reads:

For Establishment Politicians, Jim Bo Is a **Complicated** *Figure to Defend.* Is he really, or is it, rather, *uncomfortable* to stand with someone whose views are unpopular?

Similar to describing something as complicated, when it's not, is describing something as *controversial* when it's not. *Controversial* can be weaponized to mean *unacceptable*, thus shutting down the view in question. For instance:

Author Doubles Down on **Controversial View** *That Rabbits Have Delicate Hind Legs.* The follow-on to a headline like that is typically:

Fellow Author Stands up to **Controversial Author** *Amid Fallout.*

Political neutrality. Starting with "What will offend no one?" may avoid taking sides but rarely leads to the truth. A San Francisco–based nonprofit known for its prolific edits to American K–12 textbooks writes of a world history textbook: "The term 'occupied' is a politicized term inappropriate for a public school text. The text should remove it in order to be politically neutral." The ensuing passage ends up being anything but neutral.

According to. Mentioning a source in passing can create a sense of objective authority that doesn't otherwise exist, giving the writer a degree of remove—"I just told it like I heard it!" The result can still be quite slanted:

According to several sources, last night's heist was carried out by rabbits. Which sources?

According to initial reports, the rabbits absconded with at least 16 bushels of carrots. Initial reports by whom?

According to a lot of evidence, essential oils can help in many ways. What evidence in particular? This line comes from a documentary in which the guest was likely referring to results of studies done on mice, and mice alone.

According to is also used to the exact opposite effect—introducing doubt where none exists:

Badgers perfected the modern carrot. According to rabbit accounts, it was rabbits who did so. One position is stated as fact, the other as mere hearsay. Similarly:

Rabbits say teenage rabbit, 13, was shot and killed by badgers. A demonstrably objective fact is presented as a mere point of view.

In a revision to a GCSE (high school) textbook, the line "International law states that a country cannot annex or indefinitely occupy territory gained by force" was revised to read:

Some argue *that international law states that a country cannot annex or indefinitely occupy territory gained by force.* It's not like international law is a bunch of scribbles on a scrap of paper, tucked away in a poet's nightstand.

In a *Newsweek* op-ed, we read:

The scenario has existed before. It will be repeated again. Our enemy wages a war of attrition—or, **as observers of asymmetrical warfare have called it**, *the war of the flea. The flea is small and the dog is large, but over time enough attacks by enough fleas will bring down the dog. An intractable enemy must be destroyed. . . . If the dog is to survive, then the fleas must be destroyed in their earliest stages.* This author is not *really* saying an entire ethnic group is akin to fleas that must be preemptively exterminated, you see. That's just what the literature says. What can he do?

Quotations versus "scare quotes." Because quote marks can be used (factually) to cite a source and also (snarkily) to cast doubt on something, we sometimes find them used ambiguously. They can make viewpoints that aren't at all controversial seem suspect, while craftily coming across as objective. For instance:

The protestors attempted to hold **"a prayer vigil"** *at City Hall and were arrested.*

After the politician won the election, there was a big debate over the role **"identity politics"** *played in his victory.*

*Sea Turns Red in Faroe Islands as 250 Whales Slaughtered in **"Barbaric"** Hunt.* The reader is left unsure whether the author is going for subtext, irony, or a silent protest. Does the last headline insinuate that the hunt was not barbaric? Is it a quotation? Is the author in doubt about its being barbaric?

Plausible deniability? Posing opinions as questions, or phrasing them inconclusively, also lets writers off the hook for implicit assertions. For instance:

__Who__ is likely to gain from a heist on the central bank? __Will__ the world ever forgive rabbits __if__ it turns out they had a hand in it? Is this Twitter user taking a side on this issue? If he was, would he say so? Which side might that be?

An author and podcast host writes, at a time of exceptionally high anti-rabbit sentiment:

__If__ rabbits' leaders ever master the science of turning carrots into fuel, we __may be__ forced to launch a nuclear first strike against all rabbits. Needless to say, this would be an unthinkable crime, but it __may be__ the only course of action available to us. He may not *really* be saying we ought to obliterate every last rabbit. You and I are merely inferring that from his words, the way they are arranged into sentences, and what those sentences may mean.

He writes elsewhere, in a blog post:

We should profile rabbits, or anyone who looks like he or she __could conceivably be__ a rabbit, and we should be honest about it. And, again, I wouldn't put someone who looks like me __entirely__ outside the bull's-eye . . . although __I don't think__ I look like a rabbit. The second line doesn't quite sit well. What exactly is our friend saying with that farrago of words? That he ought to be profiled, maybe?

Three days later, an addendum reveals the whole point of that caveat-laden line—to lay the groundwork for deniability:

When I speak of profiling "rabbits, or anyone who looks like he or she could conceivably be a rabbit," I am not narrowly focused on mammals with long ears and protruding teeth. In fact, I included myself in the description of the type of mammal I think should be profiled.

The desire to merely *appear* rational, or to appeal to the rational, leads to this most contemptible type of dissembling—seemingly benign, but in truth deeply destructive. It pollutes our discourse, sows cognitive dissonance in the reader, and is the chosen method of a disproportionate number of people whose broad reach allows them to influence public opinion.

An Illustrated Book of Loaded Language

6. LANGUAGE THAT STARTS THE CLOCK OF HISTORY WHEN IT'S MOST CONVENIENT

Near the end of Chekhov's "The Student," the protagonist, Ivan, warming his hands in front of a fire on a bitter cold winter night, finishes a story about Peter the Apostle. The woman opposite him, having listened intently, smiles, then weeps. Ivan has an epiphany: "'The past,' he thought, 'is linked with the present by an unbroken chain of events flowing one out of the other.' And it seemed to him that he had just seen both ends of the chain; that when he touched one end the other quivered."

Language that decides unilaterally when to start or stop time does not recognize this chain of causality. Insincerely, it absolves or assigns blame, elevates or denigrates, guilts or gaslights. You can try this with any old fairy tale, to great effect. From *English Fairy Tales,* we might begin "The Story of the Three Bears" like so:

Up she started, and when she saw the Three Bears on one side of the bed, she tumbled herself out at the other, and ran to the window. Poor Goldilocks—pause for effect—to be frightened half to death by those scary bears!

Or, from *Grimms' Fairy Tales,* we might start the story of Hansel and Gretel like so:

"Stupid goose," said the old woman. "The opening is big enough. See, I myself could get in." And she crawled up and stuck her head into the oven.

Then Gretel gave her a shove, causing her to fall in. Then she closed the iron door and secured it with a bar. The old woman began to howl frightfully. But Gretel ran away, and the godless witch burned up miserably. Ignoring the egregious imagery of a witch burning to a crisp (nighty night, children), this excerpt recasts little Gretel as the murderous offender and the witch as merely a hapless victim.

This may all seem obvious, but it's truly surprising how often we find history retold with this type of selective recall. Let's look at some examples.

Where to begin . . . The following question appeared in an online lesson by the education company Studies Weekly:

What was the language used by American Indians, **many years ago***?*

The choices were: *German*, *English*, *Spanish*, and ***There was no language***.

There are a host of big problems here, as ably pointed out by Dr. Debbie Reese—the galling ignorance of *there was no language* perhaps foremost among them. But note the setting: a mythic-sounding *many years ago*, yet seemingly *after* North America was colonized by English speakers. Did history begin in the sixteenth century? Did Indigenous peoples somehow not exist before then? The past tense of *used* is also interesting, since a reader wouldn't be faulted for inferring that the language and the people who *once* existed don't exist *today*.

On SFGate, we find the headline:

Is San Francisco About to Return to Its Bohemian Roots? Why Bohemian, one might wonder? Why not, say, Ohlone, as one Redditor asks?

Wells Fargo's recent ad campaign ran with the tagline:

Re-established 2018. While a progressive sentiment, it does come across as a feeble attempt to overwrite a less than stellar past.

Starting in March 2020, a view often repeated from the White House held that the shutdown orders imposed by states tanked the US economy. The suggestion was that the problem *began* with the shutdown orders—not with a certain fast-spreading, deadly virus.

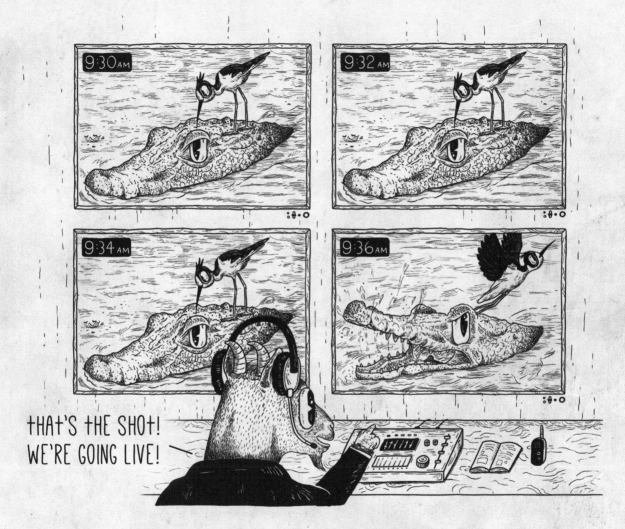

You missed a step. This cherry-picking of timelines is sometimes more blatant. In March 2020, a cable news channel reported that the World Health Organization had called masks ineffective at stopping the spread of COVID-19. The whole truth was that the WHO had already amended their previous announcement to recommend that people wear masks. The news channel chose to report the outdated guidance since it suited their narrative.

On a leading news website, we find this opening line about an agreement between nations:

The badger administration is weighing unfreezing $1 billion in funds that the rabbits' country could use for humanitarian relief, amid negotiations for badgers to reenter the multilateral deal and bring rabbits back into compliance with its terms. Of note here is that the badgers broke the agreement, unilaterally, *before* the rabbits fell out of compliance. The latter is referenced, the former isn't.

The Tower of London's website includes this description of one of the largest cut diamonds in the world:

*The history of the Koh-i-Nûr (or "Mountain of Light") diamond is steeped in myth and anecdote. Discovered in 15th-century India, it was passed from ill-fated male hand to hand, until it earned a reputation of bringing bad luck to men. **It was presented to Queen Victoria in 1849.** It now adorns the front of . . . The Queen Mother's Crown.* Curiously absent is the campaign for control of India that culminated in 1849. The Last Treaty of Lahore surrendered the Punjab region—and the diamond—to Britain.

The historical record isn't exactly regulated by some disinterested panel, which is why one often has to approach it with an extra dose of skepticism—particularly that which is peddled by a state or a party. The last example is a case in point of how several tactics we've mentioned can collude to produce a sweet narrative, worthy of a bedtime story. *Myth and anecdote* suggest that "it's complicated"; *was presented* makes excellent use of the passive voice; and the male hands that did the *passing* and the stone that did the reputation-*earning* are both cleverly anthropomorphized.

Finders, claimers. The business of *discovering*, *claiming*, and *settling* supposedly uninhabited lands, and then shoehorning such myths into the ledger of history, is rooted in the preconception that, even if the land was already inhabited by actual, breathing souls, those souls are so insignificant that they might as well not have existed.

Such claims are often justified by the clever use of language. Children still learn that America was *discovered* in 1492 (much like Count Olaf discovers the inhabited island near the end of *A Series of Unfortunate Events*). As his ship approaches the continent, Columbus writes in his journal:

At two hours after midnight, land **appeared**. Innocuous enough, were it not for the tragic events that followed. From the perspective of the native inhabitants, of course, the land was always there. It was Columbus who appeared.

Invisible coattails. We say that Pythagoras *discovered* his namesake theorem, even though it appears on Babylonian tablets dating from several hundreds of years before him. Similarly, a piece in *The Atlantic* runs:

The **history of vaccinology goes back to the late 1700s** *when Edward Jenner developed the first vaccine, for smallpox, a turning point in the war between microbes and humans*. This overlooks that vaccinology was a refinement of variolation, an idea likely imported from Constantinople in the early 1700s.

Variolation, in turn, built on inoculation, a widespread practice in China and India during the 1500s.

Saying Marconi *invented* the radio, Edison *invented* the light bulb, Johann Zahn *invented* the camera, and so on is misleading; it diminishes the essential contributions of those who came before. It determines, unilaterally, when science began.

As Abraham Flexner puts it, "Marconi's share was practically negligible . . . Marconi was inevitable. The real credit for everything that has been done in the field of wireless belongs, as far as such fundamental credit can be definitely assigned to anyone, to Professor Clerk Maxwell, who in 1865 carried out certain abstruse and remote calculations in the field of magnetism and electricity."

Invention stories are so often dramatized in popular culture that we commonly find overstatements like this one by Neil deGrasse Tyson, about a hero of his:

*Newton **invented** calculus practically on a dare.*

In the frightening territory that is the YouTube comments section, under a video that references a Zen saying, a commentor objects: "For anyone who's interested, 'You can't step in the same river twice,' isn't a Zen saying, it's Heraclitus."

Another replies:

*It is Zen **in essence**, not in origin.*

The misattribution in the video was likely accidental, but the reasoning in the second comment is troubling when applied generally: It lays the groundwork for an after-the-fact appropriation of ideas, known authorship notwithstanding.

How did we get here? A tidy narrative about fighting for some social good can distract us from how an injustice or conflict arose in the first place. Sometimes, the apparent hero of the "happy ending" is complicit in the (willfully?) forgotten cause.

A tech CEO tweets:

There is profound anti-rabbit injustice in our society. I am committing $500,000 to help alleviate some of that inequality. There's nothing wrong with a sentiment like that. Someone making a significant donation to charity is, practically speaking, a very good thing. When that person has gotten to where he is through hard work, that is a very good thing as well. But the question of how that wealth, and therefore influence, were acquired doesn't always come up. Nor, as Michael Sandel reminds us, do the deeper moral questions about the social and historical factors that advantage one person over another. Beyond the "simple solution" of *noblesse oblige*, the more imperative question is whether there is something fundamentally dysfunctional about a society that produces such a tremendous disparity.

History is particularly rife with examples of this sort. Attempting a moral case for imperialism, Arthur Balfour stated in 1910:

*Is it or is it not a good thing for these great nations . . . that this absolute government should be exercised by us? I think it is a good thing. I think that experience shows that **they have got under it a far better government** than in the whole history of the world they ever had before. . . . We are in Egypt not merely for the sake of the Egyptians, though **we are there for their sake** . . .*

Another line, from 1947, comes to mind, in which the then-head of the British Empire stated that the British Commonwealth would not fail its former colonies (which had just declared independence) in *upholding democratic principles.* Here, one feels compelled to point out: "But Your Majesty, it was your empire that hindered them from upholding those principles for over a century."

Not too long ago, a head of state proclaimed:

We did not charge hundreds of miles . . . and pay a bitter cost in casualties, and liberate 25 million rabbits, only to retreat . . . We will help them **establish a peaceful and democratic country.** The inevitable question is, did they collectively ask you to, sir? If so, we ought to question the thinking of anyone who asks for a liberation so tremendously hard to bear.

Gaslighting, a form of psychological manipulation, makes you doubt your recollection of an event, and therefore your sanity. Thus, rewriting history is an effective tool for someone who wants to stay in power, or a speaker who wants to disorient and confuse an opponent or an audience.

A panelist in a debate who spends his allotted time shouting at his opponent, when criticized for his demeanor, replies:

I apologize ***if you felt like*** *I was shouting at you.*

Guilting—emotional manipulation that aims to shift blame and steer the target in a particular direction—often follows. The gaslighter denies that past wrongs happened, then criticizes the victim for being upset. In an interview about postmodernism, a public intellectual gripes:

All these people ever talk about is oppression. Everything to them is some form of oppression. ***It's so annoying.***

James Baldwin, giving a speech in 1960s Harlem, recalls a question he hears from both friends and critics:

But ***why are you so bitter*** *all the time, Jimmy?*

In a 2017 interview, an influential author and political commentator shares:

I met Jim Bo one night, during a debate, and the first thing I realized is **how bitter he was**. *And how much he hated this country*. Although there is a sliver of truth in the idea that resentment is unproductive and even destructive, these statements' ultimate aim is to discourage voicing any concern that borders on critical, for fear of coming across as annoying, bitter, or hateful. They burden the underdog with having to second-guess himself every time a legitimate grievance about power dynamics arises. They principally serve to corner the iron-willed into silent endurance—akin to a prison guard complaining that he, too, feels imprisoned.

Gaslighting can also occur in real time. One can only imagine how confused the North African rabbits must have been as the conquering army moved in waving banners that read *Liberté, égalité, fraternité*. Again, liberty doesn't always mean liberty for everyone.

Law and disorder. Laws drafted in sneaky "disregard" of history, or causality, may do much more than they appear to at face value. Such laws *are* loaded language and breed still more.

A state builds a dam, and decides a few years later to clear the surrounding area. So, it passes a law that deems all houses near the dam *unlawful*, never mind that the houses came before the dam.

A state wishing to shift demographics or voting blocs, or otherwise try its hand at social engineering, may change the zoning laws of a neighborhood, then raze any homes that don't have the *necessary permits*—which those homeowners couldn't have gotten, anyway.

An Illustrated Book of Loaded Language

A state might also crack down on a protest by imprisoning every last nonviolent protestor, and then proclaim:

Look at the streets, these people are all violent. Where are their Martin Luther Kings?

It might also evict scores of families from their homes, then pass a missing-owner property law stating that *all unoccupied houses are state property*.

It might also destroy a city's media towers and infrastructure, causing many deaths, then counter allegations with:

Casualty reports are hard to verify because the rabbits control the media in the city.

The above are recent examples, but there's no shortage of historical cases, either:

We'll let you vote, but you have to pass a literacy test first. Oh, you can't read and write (by law)? Shame.

We'll let you vote, but you have to pay a poll tax. You can't afford it? Why ever not?

We'll let you vote, but you have to answer a brainteaser first.

The US does not have a monopoly on this sort of legal subjugation, of course—but these examples are likely familiar to most readers.

History is, as Shakespeare said of the afterlife, the land of no return. It is prone to manipulation, not least through language, to fit whatever agenda is being pushed.

In *1984*, Orwell writes, "Every record has been destroyed or falsified, every book rewritten, every picture has been repainted, every statue and street building has been renamed, every date has been altered. And the process is continuing day by day and minute by minute. History has stopped. Nothing exists except an endless present in which the Party is always right."

7. LANGUAGE THAT TELLS YOU HOW TO THINK ABOUT YOURSELF

Language is perhaps most harmful on an individual level when a person in power gets to tell you who you are. Their words burrow into our emotional state, perhaps even affecting our self-worth. As we've seen, language can deny to a group that they ever had a history, or imply that they somehow exist *outside* of history. If you think you have nothing to be proud of, you'll very likely end up feeling dislocated and dispirited.

In a 1961 broadcast, an ex-attorney general, brother to the then-president, says:

There's no question that . . . in the next thirty or forty years a rabbit can achieve the same position that my brother has. Being disenfranchised means that even the most emancipating voices often implicitly remind you that you're at such a disadvantage. Say you wanted to become the president—then maybe, in forty years' time, if the stars align and the westerly wind blows, you might be able to. The essential question here is: What must a rabbit have felt, listening to those words? How would they shape a rabbit's view of himself?

James Baldwin paints a telling picture for us: "They were not in Harlem when this statement was first heard. And they'll not hear, and possibly will never hear the laughter and the bitterness, and the scorn with which this statement was greeted. From the point of view of the man in the Harlem barber shop, Bobby Kennedy only got here yesterday, and he's already on his way to the presidency."

On the flip side, language can give you the sense that you've somehow peaked, either as an individual or as a group, and therefore have no more room to grow. We see this when labels like *developing* and *developed* are applied to nations and societies. Where does one go from *developed*? How does change continue to happen when one is brought up in a world that views itself as done?

We find the same constrictive effect when, in intellectual or religious circles, certain books are called *seminal, fully authentic*, or something to that effect, and deemed beyond reproach. In the latter case especially, such language closes the gate of curiosity. With seemingly nothing left to discover, institutions fail to adapt to changing times, stagnate, and eventually decline.

Who are you? Labels can become self-fulfilling prophecies that directly impact how a person, or group member, sees themself—and even behaves. People turn into their labels, compelled by language. Language that creates a sinister or negative group image can lead to a sense of fatalism that devours the spirit more effectively than all the tanks in the world. Consider *slave* versus *enslaved person*. Referring to people as *slaves* creates the impression of a naturally occurring group. But of course it is not a choice to be a slave, nor a genetic disposition one is born into. One is rather *enslaved*—that is, subjected to unconscionable abuse by another person.

A president responsible for dropping atomic bombs on two cities, killing at least a third of their inhabitants, wrote on August 11, 1945:

*The only language rabbits seem to understand is the one we have been using to bombard them. When you have to deal **with a beast** you have to treat him **as a beast**. It is most regrettable but nevertheless true.*

What are we supposed to do?, is the implicit sentiment. *They are beasts, after all.* The moral question of whether it is permissible to annihilate them is, a priori, put to rest. But the more times a *rabbit* listens to that broadcast, or reads those words, or watches talking heads on TV deconstructing them, the more likely that rabbit will eventually believe that, *yes, it must be so, I am a beast deserving of contempt.*

Names can also be shackling—which is exactly why Native American children, sent to "boarding schools" for reeducation, were assigned new, English names. In a particular kingdom, to this day, a newborn's name cannot be added to the civil registry if it identifies that newborn's social group too strongly. This policy creates a generation of newborns whose most identifiable signifier (their names) are the same as their rulers'—and thus, the shackling begins.

Conversely, the simple act of changing one's *own* name might allow one to reclaim a repressed identity. Examples are plenty: Oodgeroo Noonuccal (born Kathleen Ruska) is just one that comes to mind.

Place names, similarly, can imply who we belong to, or how much we matter. Naming countries after families conflates the two. Naming regions in relation to centers of power can diminish the people who live there. *North Africa* is a fair descriptor of a geographic position within a named continent; a term like *Far East*, however, is quite different. "Far from what?" one might ask, "and east of where?" Of itself, a label might not hold any subtext, but when an area is made synonymous with some degenerate quality, it becomes poisonous.

Project, slum. Words like these exemplify how language can be weaponized to exacerbate injustice. People born into *slums* may learn to think that they are incapable of social or economic mobility, and that the half-working streetlights, filthy sidewalks, and decrepit houses are somehow their lot, or of their own doing. And even when you're fired up to make a difference—how can you unstick a label that other people stuck to you?

Suppose, by law, your neighborhood is only allowed twelve hours of water a week, and the neighborhood across the street is allowed all the water it wants. It's obvious to you why *their* front yards are lush and green, and yours aren't. But to passersby, or someone born a generation or two after the law was passed, it may not be as obvious—the difference might seem to be somehow inherent in each group.

Attempts to build affordable housing in expensive cities are sometimes opposed on the grounds that they would turn the neighborhood into a *ghetto* or *slum*, or even a *high-rise slum*, as spotted in one op-ed. Fear of change isn't entirely irrational, but rather than ask the practical question of how families with different means might share a residential block, we fall back on the disquieting sentiment that people ought to stay "in their place." To quote Baldwin yet again, "It's called a *ghetto* because you can't get out of it."

But where are you really from? This expression presumes it's self-evident which geographic region someone belongs to. But history has "deposited in you an infinity of traces," as Gramsci writes in his *Prison Notebooks*. Deciding where someone is *from* thus requires picking an arbitrary beginning, which comedian Stewart Lee brilliantly deconstructs by imagining how things might have gone down 400 million years ago, had the tetrapods with barely developed lungs been told to "get back into the sea" as they crawled onto land for the very first time. *Where are you really from?* is thus a "polite" way of saying *Why don't you look like me?*

I can imagine how you feel. In an announcement about a series of layoffs, a CEO's email to all employees reads:

*We are reducing the size of the workforce by approximately 250 roles. I know that this will take a while to process. Each of us will go through **our own cycle of surprise, grief, and individual response**.* It's unlikely that this announcement comes as a *surprise to* the CEO, or that the CEO's *grief* compares to that of a person losing his or her job. But crucially (in addition to taking the edge off this one-sided decision), the implied equivalence effectively tells the employees how they *ought* to deal with this development.

Other times in corporate culture or politics, we find sentiments like:

*We're all a **family** here.* Here too, the implied equivalence with one's actual family aims to suggest how one ought to deal with the arrangement. But if your father were to have trouble drafting an email late at night, you wouldn't tell him you'll take a look at it the next morning, now would you?

Another employee might hear from her boss:

*I'm trying my best to get your promotion approved, since **I know how important that is to you**.* Is the promotion a favor, intended to placate some feeling the employee seemingly has, one might ask, or is it rather an objective reward for hard work?

In an interview with a peace broker between rabbits and badgers, we hear:

*The rabbits have an offer on the table. Whenever they decide that they want to live better lives, I believe that they will engage. We can't want peace for them **more than they want it for themselves**.* It's not hard to imagine we would uncover other factors at play, if we looked beyond this seemingly psychic diagnosis of rabbit sentiment.

An article in a leading magazine reads:

*A recent poll shows that **rabbits are happy** with how badgers treat them.* As a rabbit, I feel the need to paraphrase a colleague of mine here: Neither have these pollsters met the rabbits I have met, nor have I met the rabbits they have met.

Re-presentation. To represent is to re-present. In fiction, the integrity of the characters depends on the author's grasp of other people's lives and worldviews. In Faulkner's *Requiem for a Nun*, for instance, we meet a condemned nursemaid, Nancy. When asked what she will do once she gets to Heaven, she replies, "I can work." The clearly manufactured insinuation is that some people are so made that they will gladly work for someone else, for free, their entire lives. No matter the time or place. No matter the universe.

Historical events like Independence Day and Thanksgiving force us to reckon with wildly opposing human experiences. Independence for whom? And from whom? Often, a single outlook comes to dominate the narrative. From the perspective of the settlers who landed near Plymouth Rock, the first Thanksgiving was a peaceful, joyous exchange of food. From the Native American perspective, it marked the beginning of something very different. In *King of the Hill*, Hank asks John Redcord, "So do you celebrate Thanksgiving?"

"We did," Redcord answers. "Once."

We see re-presentation at its worst when the members of an outgroup are routinely, collectively painted in a reductive or negative light. Thus bias becomes "truth." In an interview with a top podcaster, a stand-up comedian shares the shrewd insight:

*You know how with rabbits, a lot of them **aren't really that funny**. I mean, it's not a big part of their culture, is comedy [sic]. Seinfeld thinks it's because we badgers have a love of language.*

Elsewhere, articles about the 2020 democratic primary suggest that young people don't show up to vote because they're unreliable, lazy, apathetic, naive, or, as one opinion columnist puts it, because they have *coddled minds and censorious manner and [the] inability to understand the way the world works.* Unpacking the data is one thing, and such analysis ought to take a disinterested tone. But phrases like these reinforce preconceptions about an entire group, creating a destructive sense of fatalism and possibly leading young readers to actually believe that all young people are, and always will be, lazy.

In *Eat, Pray, Love*, we read:

*I want to go where I can **marvel at something**.* Faraway lands are often painted as otherworldly, exotic, and mysterious, filled with monsters and secrets to be *marveled at*—places to *find yourself*, rather than to meet new people. (Sometimes these lands and their people are mentioned in the past tense, which reinforces the implication that they are stuck in time, ripe for marveling.)

An online tabloid published an erroneous headline, reading:

Airstrikes from Rabbits Destroy 18 Bushes, Including Eight Seedlings. A few minutes later, it realized that the exact opposite was true, and badgers were the perpetrators. Instead of fixing the headline, the paper changed it to:

***Rabbits** Launch New Attack on Badgers.* What this tells readers, and rabbits by extension, is that aggression is endemic in rabbits. It doesn't matter what they did, or had done to them. In every situation, irrespective of context or facts, they will be projected as the aggressor.

We find categorical characterizations in intellectual-sounding discourse as well, often the kind that is (ironically) a veil for anti-intellectualism. A prominent panelist comments on the challenges of integrating disparate groups into society on the Badger continent:

The only place where rabbits can have a good life is where rabbits aren't in power. In other words, in places where rabbits don't make the society. All rabbits want to have a good life. Where is the good life? Where rabbits don't determine anything.

Elsewhere, that same panelist generalizes:

In the Rabbit world, you either have one mammal eating everyone or you have free enterprise, where everyone eats everyone. That's just their culture there.

And again:

How can you coexist with these rabbits whose culture is to dunk their firstborns into a vat of carrot juice? It is their culture. This is the culture of the mainstream in the Rabbit world. Many of them do exactly that to their firstborns.

It's sweet when someone else gets to essentialize you, to deem a litany of barbarous qualities to be inherent in you—in this case, in the entire rabbit population. Although, our mustachioed academic friend—in a moment of revelatory clarity, it seems—does climb down a bit from *mainstream* to *many*.

A little bit of curiosity about others can go a long way in disabusing someone of these preconceptions.

Well, that was depressing! I hope any gloom you may feel will be short, and followed by many invigorating questions and critical inquiries. Many of us, driven to make a difference in the world, will, at some point in our lives, run up against others' preconceptions about us. I'm not sure that this proclivity can be entirely eliminated: Modeling the world as in-out groups, and broadly assigning characteristics to each, is neither a local phenomenon nor a novel one. It's ill intent that makes this insidious, parasitic even—as we've seen throughout this chapter, and indeed this whole book. The key, I think, is to recognize the impact that language has on our relationship with ourselves and our identity, and to use that heightened sensitivity to remain self-aware, confident, and independent in our thinking.

> He said a cover is not the book
> So open it up and take a look
> 'Cause under the covers one discovers
> That the king may be a crook
> Chapter titles are like signs
> And if you read between the lines
> You'll find your first impression was mistook
> For a cover is nice, but a cover is not the book
>
> —*Marc Shaiman and Scott Wittman,*
> Mary Poppins Returns

THE FIRST TETRAPOD.

FINAL REMARKS

I first heard the saying "walls have ears" when I was very young, seven or eight probably. The upshot was clear: Be careful what you say, and if you do risk saying it, don't *really* say it. The reading of poetry and novels takes new form once you're equipped with hypersensitivity to subtext—poetry in particular. So many verses that seemed benign were in fact, I came to realize, loaded with political subtext. Even nursery rhymes: *"Baa Baa, Black Sheep" is poking fun at king and country, I see!*

Taken in one direction, this awareness becomes a potent weapon for dissent in a hostile environment. One can use language (or write books with furry animals in them) to get a point across without, ideally, losing any of one's limbs.

If taken in another direction, however, it becomes something quite oppressive, quite ugly. A state might use it to escape any kind of accountability. Rather than subjugate some targeted group extrajudicially—thus putting itself in the position of having to mount a moral defense of its actions—a state might pass any legislation it wants, and then lean on those laws when it needs to. Law is law, after all, one is told.

Similarly, a populist might use subtext to dog-whistle at his supporters—to hide bigotry in plain sight, behind a veneer of plausible deniability. Therefore, when cornered, he feels neither legally nor morally compelled to admit his intent.

The precariousness of the present time in America is not lost on me—of this year, and likely of the years to come. I have felt its heat up close, as I'm sure many others have as well. The orthodoxy that yesterday might have been dismissed as fringe, as merely rhetorical, today proves capable of mobilizing devoted believers to destructive ends. As the political cycle nears its next frenzied zenith, one can only expect the viciousness of the rhetoric, the scapegoating, the tribalism—the general anger and animosity that make up so much of political discourse—to increase.

Whether we like it or not, our lives are intertwined with politics and political discourse. As critical thinkers, we must not shy away from it; we must bring to it the much-needed quality of truth-telling. As C. Wright Mills puts it, "it is in politics that intellectual solidarity and effort must be centered. If the thinker does not relate himself to the value of truth in political struggle, he cannot responsibly cope with the whole of live experience."

In this book, you'll have noticed, I didn't spend a lot of time on obvious mistruths or outright lies, on the clearly prejudiced or the clearly emotive. Saying you have "alternative facts" is silly. Subtler examples, I find, are much more interesting: They're more insidious, and require greater courage to point out.

The introduction begins with a discussion of cognitive biases: Often, we focus more on whether we like someone than on the truth of their message. That's where the idea of not naming publications (for the most part), and obscuring individuals and groups with animals came from—to let readers see around whatever bias they may have.

The paradox, of course, is that I have my own. The media I read most, and the people I listen to most, and the world events I'm most attuned to, end up being my source material. When I cite them, it's by no means to enshrine them as infallible—and when I criticize them, it's not at all to dismiss them as categorically unreliable.

Having said and done that, my hope is that this book will help us not only recognize insincerity, but also better deal with what's likely to come. By tuning our senses to the *subtlest* patterns of sneaky rhetoric, we'll hopefully make it second nature to recognize and reveal rhetoric that is more vitriolic, more brazen—and so often, all too effective.

So raise your rabbit ears to listen for what's left unsaid: What's missing from this narrative? To whose benefit? Is a tribalistic quality like someone's identity, or whose side they're on, being offered up as proof of their goodness or believability? What does this tell me about the writer's point of view? Am I being maneuvered into hating someone or something? Into believing someone or something?

Questions I hope we'll all remember to ask.

SUGGESTED READING

Bryson, Bill. *Bryson's Dictionary of Troublesome Words*. New York: Broadway Books, 2002.

Lutz, William. *Doublespeak*. United Kingdom: Harper & Row, 1989.

Orwell, George. *1984*. London: Secker & Warburg, 1949. (Quoted on page 71.)

Orwell, George. *Orwell on Truth*. Boston: Houghton Mifflin Harcourt, 2018.

Orwell, George. "Politics and the English Language." London: *Horizon*, 1946. (Quoted in this book on pages 6 and 32.)

Queneau, Raymond. *Exercises in Style*. Translated by Barbara Wright. New York: New Directions, 1981.

Rogers, Todd and Michael I. Norton. "The Artful Dodger." Harvard Business School Working Knowledge, Harvard University, Boston, MA, September 2008. hbswk.hbs.edu/item/the-artful-dodger-answering-the-wrong-question-the-right-way.

SOURCES

That the very concept, page viii. George Orwell. "Looking Back on the Spanish War." London: *New Road*, 1943.

The classic example of framing, page 2. Amos Tversky and David Kahneman. "The Framing of Decisions and the Psychology of Choice." *Science* 211.4481 (1981): 453–458.

Many of my critics, page 14. Sam Harris. *The Moral Landscape*. New York: Simon & Schuster, 2010.

Closer to home, page 16. "Whatever Happened to Global Warming?" *The Daily Mail*, October 14, 2009.

Once in every generation, page 19. J. M. Coetzee. *Waiting for the Barbarians: A Novel*. New York: Penguin Books, 1980.

In the midst, page 27. "Elect Joe Biden, America." *The New York Times*, October 7, 2020.

Concerns investment rather than trade, page 30. Duncan Green. *The Silent Revolution*. New York: Monthly Review Press, 2003.

Those in the pro-us, page 40. Thomas L. Freidman. "A Geopolitical Earthquake Just Hit the Mideast." *The New York Times*, August 13, 2020.

General interference, page 40. *Simple Sabotage Field Manual*. United States Office of Strategic Services, 1944. hsdl.org/?abstract&did=750070.

We make to ourselves pictures, page 42. Ludwig Wittgenstein. *Tractatus Logico-Philosophicus*. Translated by C. K. Ogden. London: Kegan Paul, Trench, Trübner & Co., 1922.

Mobile army, page 42. Friedrich Nietzsche. "On Truth and Lies in a Nonmoral Sense." 1896.

Language, incontestably, page 47. James Baldwin. "If Black English Isn't a Language, Then Tell Me, What Is?" *The New York Times*, July 29, 1979.

You just might end up richer, page 48. Jessica Stillman. "Bill Gates Always Reads Before Bed. Science Suggests You Should Too." Inc.com, April 14, 2020.

Ultimately, the grown-ups, page 52. "U.S. Congress's Dereliction of Leadership on Government Shutdown." *The Washington Post*, September 29, 2013.

The scenario has existed before, page 58. Abraham Miller. "In the Middle East, Give War a Chance." *Newsweek*, May 19, 2021.

The past, he thought, page 61. Anton Chekhov. *The Witch and Other Stories*. Translated by Constance Garnett. New York: Macmillan, 1918.

The history of vaccinology, page 65. Alan Bernstein. "I'm Optimistic That We Will Have a COVID-19 Vaccine Soon." *The Atlantic*, August 29, 2020.

Marconi's share, page 66. Abraham Flexner. "The Usefulness of Useless Knowledge." *Harper's Magazine*, June/November 1939.

They were not in Harlem, page 72. James Baldwin, debating William F. Buckley. Cambridge University's Union Hall. February 18, 1965. youtube.com/watch?v=oFeoS41xe7w.

Deposited in you an infinity of traces, page 75. Antonio Gramsci. *Prison Notebooks*. New York: Columbia University Press, 2011.

Coddled minds, page 78. Bret Stephens. "Dear Millennials: The Feeling Is Mutual." *The New York Times*, May 17, 2019.

It is in politics, page 83. C. Wright Mills. *The Politics of Truth*. New York: Oxford University Press, 2008.

An Illustrated Book of Loaded Language

ACKNOWLEDGMENTS

An Illustrated Book of Loaded Language is illustrated by my good friend and longtime collaborator Alejandro Giraldo. The best out there, bar none. It was edited by the inimitable Karen Giangreco. I'm truly in awe of the breadth of her expertise, and how much the book is better because of her care and attention. My gratitude to everyone at The Experiment, most notably, Beth Bugler for driving the cover from concept to the stunning final version, and Jack Dunnington for his work on the book's interior design.

My thanks to Grigory Pogulsky for reviewing and contributing to an early draft, and to Reed O'Brien for sharing the study on artful dodging with me. To my father for reviewing the project when it was still an outline and terribly rough around the edges. To two anonymous reviewers for contributing significant edits to the work's first translated edition online. To Irina "Alex" Sandu for contributing excellent examples to several sections. To the cafes in downtown San Francisco, inside which (and outside which, due to the pandemic) much of this book took shape. To my daughter, Fatima, for her writing, which continues to inspire me. And to all the readers of my books, all the subscribers to my mailing list, and everyone who has shared my work with others. For your tremendous support, I'm grateful. This project is the first of two companions to *An Illustrated Book of Bad Arguments*.

ABOUT THE AUTHOR AND ILLUSTRATOR

Ali Almossawi's first book, *An Illustrated Book of Bad Arguments*, has been enjoyed by over three million readers online and in print. He holds a masters in engineering systems from the Massachusetts Institute of Technology (MIT) and a masters in software engineering from Carnegie Mellon University. Ali has worked at Harvard, where his research involved creating predictive models of source code quality, and at the MIT Media Lab, where he contributed to data visualization projects. His work has appeared in several publications, including *Scientific American*, *Wired*, and *Fast Company*. He lives in San Francisco with his wife and daughter.

Almossawi.com
BookofBadArguments.com

Alejandro Giraldo holds a degree in graphic design from UPB Medellín and a masters in art direction from ELISAVA (the Barcelona School of Design and Engineering). He runs the clothing company Velmost and works as a freelance illustrator. He lives in Medellín, Colombia.

AlejoGiraldo.com